ANIMALS
ANIMALS

MONKEYS

BY MELISSA McDANIEL

BENCHMARK **B**OOKS

MARSHALL CAVENDISH
NEW YORK

Series Consultant
James G. Doherty
General Curator, Bronx Zoo, New York

Benchmark Books
Marshall Cavendish
99 White Plains Road
Tarrytown, NY 10591–9001
www.marshallcavendish.com

Library of Congress Cataloging–in–Publication Data

McDaniel, Melissa.
Monkeys / by Melissa McDaniel.
p. cm.–(Animals, animals)
Summary: Describes the life of monkeys, including social structure, reproduction and child
rearing, diet, interaction with humans, and loss of habitat.
Includes bibliographical references and index.
ISBN 0-7614-1615-3
1. Monkeys–Juvenile literature. [1. Monkeys.] I. Title. II. Series.
QL737.P9M4 2003   599.8–dc21
2003001837

Photo research by Anne Burns Images

Cover Photo by Visuals Unlimited/Beth Davidow

All the photographs in this book are used with permission and through the courtesy of:
Animals Animals: Zig Leszczynski, 4; J.& P. Wegner, 11; Patti Murray, 12; Gerard Lacz, 14–15; J. & P. Wegner, 18 (top left); Dani/Jeske, 18
(bottom); B. & B. Wells, OSF, 18 (bottom); E. Parker, OSF, 19 (bottom); Barbara von Hoffmann, 25; Miriam Agron, 26–27; Anup Shah, 30;
Werner Layer, 33; Patti Murray, 34–35; Shane Moore, 38; J.Downer, OSF, 41.
Peter Arnold: Martin Harvey, 9; Fred Bruemmer, 36; Kevin Schaefer, 42.
Visuals Unlimited: Rob Simpson, 18 (center right); Ken Lucas, 19 (center left); Milton H.Tierney Jr, 22.

Printed in China

1 3 5 6 4 2

Front Cover: A mother squirrel monkey carries her baby.

CONTENTS

babys

1 INTRODUCING MONKEYS

High in the treetops a monkey leaps from a branch. Flying through the air, its arms and legs are thrust forward while its tail hangs below. The monkey lands, balances briefly with its tail and then starts again, jumping 20 feet (6 meters) to the next tree. It grabs a branch with strong flexible hands and calls out *"eeh-oh-oh-oh-oh-oh-oh."* Nothing says jungle like the cry of a monkey.

Monkeys are amazing acrobats. They have long, strong arms and legs that they use to swing, leap, and bounce from branch to branch. The red colobus monkey can jump down more than 60 feet (18 m) and then use the branch it lands on as a springboard to its next perch. Another type of monkey, the pied colobus, can jump down more than 150 feet (46 m) from treetops to lower branches without hurting itself.

A SPIDER MONKEY GRABS A TREE BRANCH WITH ITS STRONG, FLEXIBLE TAIL.

MONKEYS VARY GREATLY IN SIZE. PYGMY MARMOSETS ARE BETWEEN 7 AND 12 INCHES (15 CENTIMETERS) LONG, NOT INCLUDING THE TAIL. MANDRILLS CAN GROW TO NEARLY 3 FEET (1 METER) TALL.

Monkeys belong to a larger group called *primates* that include apes–and you. A lot of people say monkey when they are actually talking about great apes such as chimpanzees or orangutans. So what is the difference between an ape and a monkey? The most obvious difference is that monkeys have tails, and apes do not. Apes are bigger than monkeys, and they also have larger brains. This allows apes to perform very complex tasks.

Still, monkeys are among the smartest animals. They are able to solve problems and teach what they have learned to others in their groups. One Japanese macaque began washing her sweet potatoes before she ate them to keep from getting sand in her mouth. Within a few months, all the other macaques in her group were doing the same thing.

Monkeys can act on their smarts because they have flexible fingers and toes. Many *mammals* have short, stiff fingers and toes with claws on the end. This may be good for running and fighting, but these creatures cannot easily pick up a sweet potato to wash it. Many monkeys also have what is called an *opposable thumb*, like humans do. This means they can move the thumb so it is opposite any of their fingers, forming a circle. Having an opposable thumb makes it easy to pick up and hold small objects such as fruit. It also helps monkeys get a good grip on tree branches.

Many monkeys live in trees. These monkeys usually have tails that are longer than the rest of their bodies. Some South American monkeys, such as spider monkeys and howlers, have tails that they can use to hold things. It is like having another hand. Most monkeys cannot grab with their tails, but their tails still help them balance on branches.

Monkeys have excellent eyesight. They have both eyes in the front of their heads, which helps them tell how far away something is. This is very important for monkeys. Sailing 20 or 30 feet (6 or 9 m) through the air, they need to be able to tell exactly how far away a branch is in order to land safely.

MONKEYS CAN PICK UP AND HOLD FOOD EASILY BECAUSE THEY HAVE LONG FINGERS AND THUMBS.

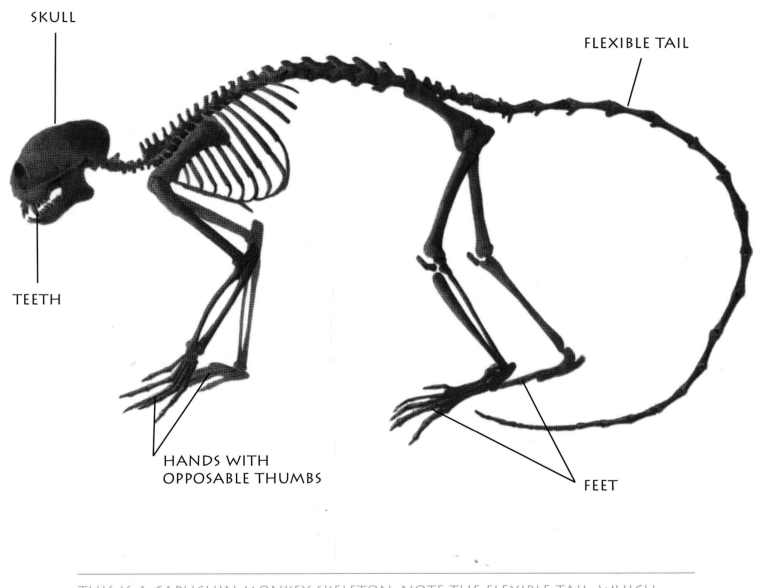

SKULL

FLEXIBLE TAIL

TEETH

HANDS WITH
OPPOSABLE THUMBS

FEET

THIS IS A CAPUCHIN MONKEY SKELETON. NOTE THE FLEXIBLE TAIL, WHICH
CAPUCHIN MONKEYS USE TO HELP BALANCE. LONG FINGERS MAKE IT EASY FOR
THE MONKEYS TO GRAB THINGS.

MONKEYS' EYES ARE IN THE FRONT OF THEIR HEADS. THIS HELPS THEM TELL EXACTLY HOW FAR AWAY SOMETHING IS.

Monkeys can also see color well. This allows them to spot ripe fruit in far-off trees. It also helps them to recognize each other. Some monkeys have brightly colored markings on their bodies. The bald uakari's entire face is bright red. Such coloring comes in handy in the thick jungles where many monkeys live.

2
A MONKEY'S WORLD

There are more than 200 *species*, or types, of monkeys in the world, ranging from the tiny marmosets of South America to the colorful mandrills of Africa. Scientists divide monkeys into two big groups, New World monkeys and Old World monkeys. New World monkeys live in Central and South America. Old World monkeys live in Asia and Africa. The only monkeys that live in Europe are some Barbary macaques that live on Gibraltar, a finger of land on Spain's southern coast.

Most monkeys live in warm, tropical areas. Only in warm regions can they get fruit and other food all year. Japanese macaques live farther north than any other primate except humans, high in the mountains of Japan. Although the region is hot in the summer, winters are cold and snowy. These macaques have much thicker fur than other monkeys.

VERVET MONKEYS SPEND SOME OF THEIR TIME IN THE TREES AND SOME ON THE PLAINS.

JAPANESE MACAQUES HUDDLE
TOGETHER IN THE SNOW.

Some of these so-called snow monkeys are lucky enough to live near hot springs, pools that have been warmed by hot underground rocks. During the frigid winters, they often take a dip in the steaming water.

All New World monkeys live in trees. Many of them spend their whole lives in the treetops, flitting from branch to branch. Most prefer thick jungles filled with vines. But some New World species have chosen to live in drier, sparser forests.

Old World monkeys live in a wider range of places. Many Old World monkeys, such as mangabeys, live in trees. Mandrills live in the forest but spend much of their time on the ground. Other Old World monkeys live in the African *savannas*, areas of grassland dotted with trees. These monkeys are well suited to life in the open. Patas

NO ONE KNOWS THE EXACT NUMBER OF MONKEY SPECIES IN THE WORLD, BECAUSE NEW ONES ARE FREQUENTLY DISCOVERED. BETWEEN 1990 AND 2002, TWENTY-FOUR NEW TYPES OF MONKEYS WERE IDENTIFIED. THESE MONKEYS HAD NOT BEEN DISCOVERED EARLIER BECAUSE FEW SCIENTISTS HAD EXPLORED THE REMOTE PARTS OF THE AMAZON JUNGLE WHERE THE MONKEYS LIVE. ONE SCIENTIST WHO DID IS MARC VAN ROOSMALEN. HE HAS DISCOVERED AS MANY AS TWENTY MONKEY SPECIES IN THE AMAZON.

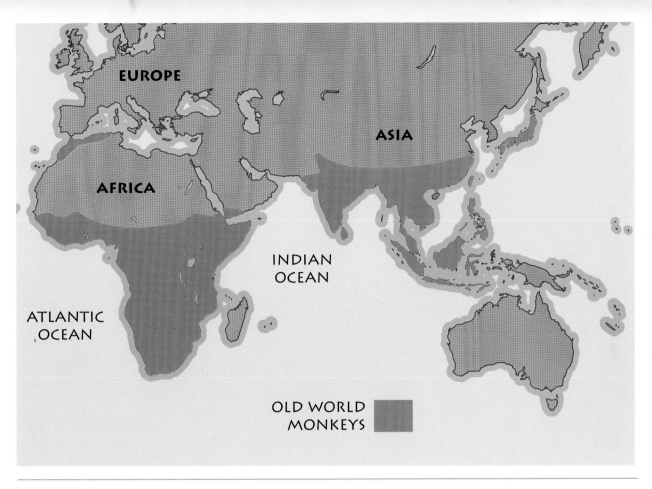

THIS MAP SHOWS WHERE OLD WORLD MONKEYS LIVE. IN AFRICA, ONLY THE MACAQUES LIVE NORTH OF THE SAHARA DESERT.

monkeys have longer legs than most other monkeys. This means that if there are no trees to climb, they can escape *predators* by running fast along the ground.

No matter where they live, most monkeys will climb trees to bed down for the night. This gives them some protection from predators that hunt at night. If there are no trees around, monkeys may look for spots on high cliffs.

MONKEY SPECIES

HERE ARE SIX TYPES OF MONKEYS AND WHERE THEY LIVE.

OLD WORLD MONKEYS

MANDRILL
WEST-CENTRAL AFRICA

BARBARY MACAQUE
NORTH AFRICA AND GIBRALTAR

LION-TAILED MACAQUE
INDIA

NEW WORLD MONKEYS

NORTHERN OWL MONKEY
VENEZUELA AND BRAZIL

PYGMY MARMOSET
SOUTH AMERICA

UAKARI
BRAZIL, COLOMBIA, PERU

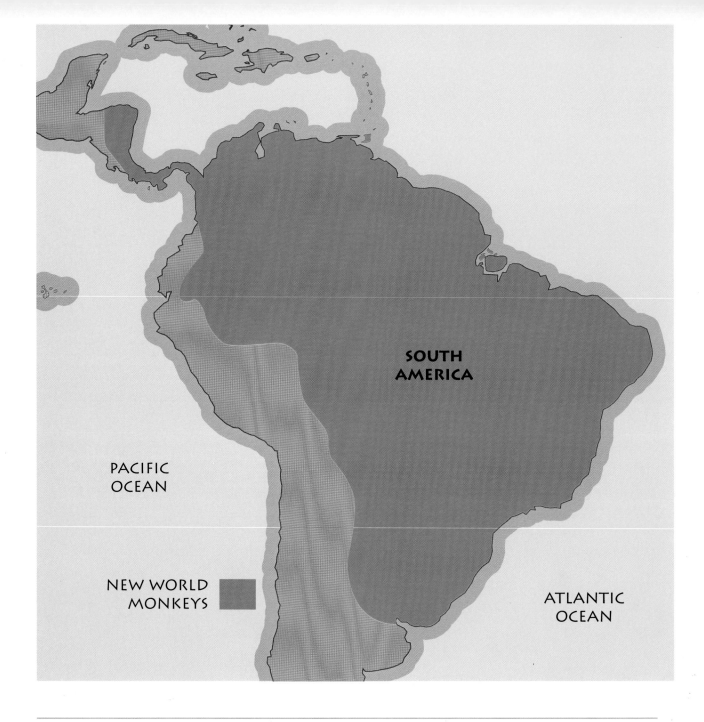

PACIFIC
OCEAN

SOUTH
AMERICA

ATLANTIC
OCEAN

NEW WORLD
MONKEYS

NEW WORLD MONKEYS LIVE IN CENTRAL AND SOUTH AMERICA. NOTICE THAT
THEY DO NOT LIVE IN THE SOUTHERN AND WESTERN PARTS OF SOUTH AMERICA.

Almost all monkeys are more active during the day than at night. The only one that is *nocturnal*, or more active at night, is the South American owl monkey, also known as the night monkey. These creatures have much larger eyes than other monkeys, so they can see better at night. But even night monkeys are not as well adapted to the dark as other animals. Unlike many night creatures, night monkeys need a little light to help them find their way around, so they are most active when there is a full moon.

3
FAMILY LIFE

When baby monkeys are born, they are more developed than their human relatives. A human baby may squeeze its mother's fingers. A baby monkey will reach out and grasp its mother's fur–and hang on. Monkeys spend the first weeks or months of their lives clinging to their mother's bellies. There, they are safe and protected. This also allows them to nurse easily.

Like all mammals, infant monkeys drink their mother's milk. Many do not begin eating solid food for a few months. This can be quite tiring for the mothers. They have to spend even more time than usual searching for food to make sure they make enough milk to feed their babies.

Monkeys are social animals. When a baby is born, other monkeys often want to get a peek at it. Mother baboons do not like this. But other types of monkeys have found that friendly interest can be helpful. Langurs,

A MALE BARBARY MACAQUE WITH A BABY FROM HIS GROUP

for instance, often let other females take care of their babies. This gives the mothers more time to rest and feed.

Monkeys stay pregnant for four to eight months, depending on the species. Because tending to a baby monkey takes so much time and effort, most monkeys have only one baby at a time. But a few types of monkeys, including tamarins and marmosets, often have twins. In these species, the father gets into the act. Tamarin and marmoset fathers carry their babies almost all of the time. The mother takes the young only to feed them. In most other monkey species, the fathers are not involved with the babies much at all.

After a few weeks or months, some baby monkeys start riding on the mother's back. They also begin to check out their surroundings. They run and jump, swing and spring. This is much of what makes monkeys so popular at the zoo. Still, the little pranksters are far from fully grown.

THE BLACK-HANDED SPIDER MONKEY HAS BEEN KNOWN TO LIVE AS LONG AS FORTY-EIGHT YEARS. SCIENTISTS BELIEVE THIS IS LONGER THAN ANY OTHER MONKEY. THE FACT IS THAT SCIENTISTS DO NOT KNOW THE LIFE SPAN OF MANY OF THE WORLD'S MONKEYS. BUT THEY DO KNOW THAT MOST LIVE LONGER IN ZOOS THAN THEY DO IN THE WILD.

WHEN THESE TINY VERVET MONKEYS GROW UP, THEY MAY WEIGH AS MUCH AS 17 POUNDS.

RED-CROWNED MANGABEYS
HELP EACH OTHER GROOM
HARD-TO-REACH PLACES.

Young monkeys rely on their mothers until they are one or two years old. Depending on the species, they are ready to have babies of their own when they are between eighteen months and six years old.

All monkeys live in groups. Some of these groups may be families made up of a male, a female, and a few offspring. Others are large groups with more than 200 monkeys. Living in groups helps protect monkeys from attack. With a lot of monkeys keeping an eye out, it is likely that one will spot a predator coming near. And if a predator does attack, a group of monkeys can sometimes scare the creature off. A lone monkey would surely be eaten.

Monkeys get more out of group life than just protection. Monkeys like being around other monkeys. One way they show this is by *grooming*. In grooming, one animal carefully cleans the fur of another, picking out the dirt, dead skin, and

SOME TYPES OF MANGABEY MONKEYS HAVE A SPECIAL WAY OF COMMUNICATING. THESE ANIMALS HAVE DARK FACES, BUT THEIR HUGE EYELIDS ARE WHITE. THE MANGABEYS SOMETIMES SIGNAL TO EACH OTHER BY BLINKING. THE OTHER MANGABEYS CAN EASILY SEE THE FLASHING WHITE LIDS.

insects. Both animals seem to find grooming very relaxing. Many baboons groom for three or four hours a day.

Grooming is just one of the many ways that monkeys communicate with each other. Monkeys hoot, howl, and cluck to pass on information. They also have very expressive faces. Opening the mouth a little bit might be a threat, while opening it in a slightly different way might mean giving in. People may not be able to tell the difference between those faces, but monkeys know just what they mean.

4
MONKEY FOOD

Picture a monkey eating. The image that pops into most people's heads is a monkey holding a banana. While it is true that many monkeys would love a banana for lunch, monkeys actually have much wider diets than this.

Some monkeys eat mainly fruit. With their good vision, they can spot ripe fruit from far off. Then they swing through the branches to reach the food. They use their nimble hands to pick the fruit, rip it open, and hold it while they eat. Some fruit eaters return to the same trees every few days to eat whatever new fruit has ripened.

Marmosets are fruit eaters. They also eat flowers and small animals such as frogs. But they specialize in eating gum, the thick, sticky material inside some trees. Marmosets have sharp bottom teeth that they use to make holes in the bark. When the gum flows out, the marmoset laps it up.

A RED COLOBUS MONKEY MUNCHES ON A TASTY LEAF.

Other monkeys eat mainly leaves. Leaf–eating monkeys have sharp ridges on their teeth and large stomachs. The ridges make it easier to chew the leaves while the large stomachs allow them to eat and digest more leaves.

Howler monkeys are leaf eaters. Because leaves are so common, these monkeys do not have to travel far for a meal. Rather than swinging through the trees looking for ripe fruit, they move slowly along the treetops, munching away at one leaf after another. Unlike fruit–eating monkeys, which tend to travel over wide areas, leaf–eating monkeys will often move less than a quarter of a mile (400 m) in a day.

A lot of monkeys also like eating nuts. Some monkeys smash the nuts against trees to get out the fleshy parts. Some monkeys, like the Saki monkeys from South America, have such strong jaws that they can crack nuts open in their mouths.

THE BLACK-AND-WHITE COLOBUS HAS STRANGE TASTE. IT IS A LEAF-EATING MONKEY, BUT IT OFTEN HEADS TO THE GROUND FOR A NICE SNACK OF DIRT. THE SOIL PROVIDES THE MONKEY WITH MINERALS THAT ARE LACKING IN LEAFY MEALS.

ONLY MALE SAKI MONKEYS HAVE THIS STRIKING WHITE FACE. THE FEMALES
ARE BROWNISH GRAY WITH ONLY A NARROW WHITE STRIPE ON THE FACE.
SAKIS RARELY GO DOWN TO THE GROUND OR CLIMB TO THE TOP OF THE
TREES. INSTEAD, THEY HOP AMONG BRANCHES AND LEAP DOWN THROUGH
GAPS. THEY ARE SOMETIMES CALLED FLYING MONKEYS.

33

HOWLER MONKEYS SPEND THEIR
DAYS MOVING THROUGH THE TREE-
TOPS EATING LEAVES. THEIR NAME
COMES FROM THEIR LOUD ROAR,
WHICH CAN BE HEARD FOR MILES.

THIS LONE OLIVE BABOON IS CONTENT TO EAT LEAVES AND GRASS, BUT LARGE GROUPS OF THESE MONKEYS SOMETIMES HUNT SMALL MAMMALS.

36

Baboons probably have more varied diets than any other monkeys. These big monkeys live across much of Africa and eat whatever they can find. Their favorite foods are fruits. But they also use their strong hands to dig up roots and seeds. Some eat grass, while others have been known to munch on water lilies. Many monkeys will eat insects, birds, eggs, and small animals such as frogs. But baboons are the only ones that hunt larger animals. They have been known to kill small antelopes.

Still, monkeys are not known as hunters. They have much more reason to fear other animals than other animals have to fear them. Many large predators find monkeys a tasty treat. Eagles may be the biggest threat to monkeys that live in trees. These powerful birds swoop in and grab monkeys from the branches. Monkeys that live on the ground have to worry about big cats such as cheetahs, leopards, and lions. Dog–like animals such as hyenas and jackals may chase down and kill monkeys.

But no matter how many times in the savanna a cheetah snatches up a monkey, cheetahs are not monkeys' worst enemies. That title belongs to the monkeys' close relatives– the humans.

5
MONKEYS AND MAN

Monkeys and their human relatives have a complicated relationship. Monkeys are among the most popular animals at zoos because they are so lively and fun loving. And since they are so much like us, there is something eerie about watching them play and fight and care for each other.

But being like us has not really helped the monkeys. Monkeys are so closely related to humans they have often been used for medical research. This has been very helpful to humans. But it has been disastrous for the monkeys. Fifty years ago, more than 200,000 monkeys were shipped to the United States each year for medical research. So many rhesus monkeys were used for research that their population in India dropped by more than 90 percent between 1958 and 1980.

CUTTING DOWN FORESTS ALONG THE COAST OF BRAZIL HAS DESTROYED MOST OF THE GOLDEN LION TAMARINS' HABITAT. TODAY, ONLY ABOUT A THOUSAND OF THESE ANIMALS REMAIN IN THE WILD.

Some monkeys are also threatened because people hunt them for food. Eating monkey meat is common in South America and Africa. Some monkey species, such as drills in Africa, have been almost entirely wiped out from hunting. Some people will pay more for this "bush meat" than for more traditional meats.

But the biggest threat monkeys face is losing their *habitat*, the places where they live. Every time someone clears another section of the Amazon rain forest in Brazil and turns it into a cattle ranch, more monkeys lose their homes. The same is true every time someone cuts down a tree in Vietnam or Nigeria to sell the wood. And as cities across the tropical world expand into the forests, monkeys are forced into smaller and smaller regions.

Some types of monkeys can handle a changing world. Many macaques seem to have adjusted to life in or close to cities. They tip over garbage cans to get food. Some even climb into people's houses. Other types of monkeys have taken advantage of farms that have been started near their homes. The red-crowned mangabeys of Africa love eating rice and corn. They raid the farms so often that some farmers consider them pests and hunt them.

RHESUS MONKEYS THAT HAVE MOVED INTO CITIES IN INDIA SEEM TO LIKE LIVING NEAR PEOPLE. IF THEY ARE RETURNED TO THE COUNTRYSIDE, THEY OFTEN FIND ANOTHER TOWN TO LIVE IN.

FEWER THAN 400 WOOLLY SPIDER MONKEYS REMAIN IN THE WILD.
HUMANS HAVE DESTROYED MORE THAN 95 PERCENT OF THE KIND OF
FOREST IT REQUIRES FOR SURVIVAL.

But many other monkeys cannot survive in changed environments. They can only get the foods they need in the forests. As their habitat disappears, so do the animals. Among the most endangered monkeys are African drills, lion-tailed macaques of India, and woolly spider monkeys and golden lion tamarins of South America.

Some people are trying to help the monkeys, but it is difficult work. Education programs have helped decrease hunting in some areas. But nothing is going to bring back the vast tracts of forest that have been carved up and cut down.

People love monkeys. They love watching them at the zoo. But as the tropical forests disappear, it is possible that zoos will be the only places that some monkeys can live. The world would be a much poorer place if never again did it see a hundred mandrills, their red-and-white faces blazing, marching together through a forest in West Africa, where they belong.

grooming: The behavior in which one animal carefully cleans the fur of another animal.

habitat: The place where a plant or animal lives.

mammals: A large class of animals that includes monkeys, humans, elephants, mice, and thousands of others. All mammals give birth to live young and nurse them with milk.

nocturnal: To be more active at night.

opposable thumb: A thumb that can be moved so it is opposite any finger, forming a circle.

primates: A group of animals that includes monkeys, apes, and humans. All primates have large brains, arms and legs that move freely, eyes that face forward, and flexible fingers and toes.

predators: Animals that hunt and eat other animals.

savannas: Tropical grasslands dotted with trees.

species: A single type of animal.

BOOKS

Arnold, Caroline. *Monkey*. New York: Morrow, 1993.

Banks, Martin. *How Monkeys "Talk."* New York: Benchmark Books, 1998.

Harmon, Amanda. *New World Monkeys*. Danbury, CT: Grolier, 2001.

Horak, Steven A. *Baboons and Other Old World Monkeys*. Chicago: World Book, 2002.

Martin, Patricia A. Fink. *Monkeys of Asia and Africa*. New York: Children's Press, 2000.

Redmond, Ian. *Gorilla, Monkey & Ape*. New York: Dorling Kindersley, 2000.

Steedman, Scott. *Amazing Monkeys*. New York: Alfred A. Knopf, 1991.

VIDEOS

A Howler Monkey Village. Stamford, CT: ABC Video, 1995.

National Geographic's Really Wild Animals: Monkey Business and Other Family Fun. Washington D. C.: National Geographic, 1996.

The Return of the Woolly Monkey. Stamford, CT: ABC Video, 1995.

WEBSITES

African Primates at Home

www.indiana.edu/~primate/primates.html

Mindy's Memory Monkey Facts

www.mindysmem.org/monkeys.html

Monkeys! Monkeys!

www.monkeys–monkeys.com/

ABOUT THE AUTHOR

Melissa McDaniel is the author of fifteen books for young people. She lives in New York City, where she and her daughter, Iris, love watching the monkeys in the Central Park Zoo.

I N D E X

Page numbers for illustrations are in **boldface.**